18 YEARS IN THE MAKING

For This Child We Prayed

Our Emotional Journey Through IVF, Fostering
and Adoption to Our Miracle Natural Conception

Leanne Davey

First published by Ultimate World Publishing 2021
Copyright © 2021 Leanne Davey

ISBN

Paperback: 978-1-922714-20-6
Ebook: 978-1-922714-21-3

Leanne Davey has asserted her rights under the Copyright, Designs and Patents Act 1988 to be identified as the author of this work. The information in this book is based on the author's experiences and opinions. The publisher specifically disclaims responsibility for any adverse consequences which may result from use of the information contained herein. Permission to use information has been sought by the author. Any breaches will be rectified in further editions of the book.

All rights reserved. No part of this publication may be reproduced, stored in or introduced into a retrieval system, or transmitted in any form, or by any means (electronic, mechanical, photocopying, recording or otherwise) without the prior written permission of the author. Any person who does any unauthorised act in relation to this publication may be liable to criminal prosecution and civil claims for damages. Enquiries should be made through the publisher.

Cover design: Ultimate World Publishing
Layout and typesetting: Ultimate World Publishing
Editor: Victoria Pickens
Photographer: Esther Muirhead

Ultimate World Publishing
Diamond Creek,
Victoria Australia 3089
www.writeabook.com.au

Dedication

Thank you to my courageous and loving husband, Ian, who has walked this path to parenthood with me. Every step of the way we have fought together for our relationship, and I love you more today than our wedding day, you have always encouraged me to fly. To each of our family members, your support and love and acceptance has held such a special place in our hearts. To our son, Zachariah, you are a dream come true and we are so blessed to have you in our lives, your cheeky smile and sense of humour brightens each and every day. To our church family and friends, thank you for your prayers and your faith in God, it has sustained us for many years. Thank You Lord that Your word is true and we have been blessed with our son.

Testimonials

"A compelling roller coaster of a read! Leanne writes in an easy-to-read way that draws the reader in as she shares the many highs and lows on her journey to fulfilling her life's mission to become a mum. As a psychologist, mum and avid reader, I recommend this book to you. Be ready to cry, laugh, and celebrate as you travel with Leanne on this epic journey!"

Sharon Hensby
Psychologist

"Leanne's story is one of pain and heartache, joy and God's faithfulness. She gives voice to a secret suffering for women/couples that helps bring insight to the journey of infertility, all the while holding onto hope and the faithfulness of God. A refreshing and hope filled story, thank you for writing this Leanne, you are a gift to many."

Kristy Godfrey
Senior Minister C3 Kingscliff

"Leanne's book is a real and thought-provoking account of the experience of infertility. However, it is more than just her experience. This book evokes compassion, joy and a deeper understanding of grief and loss regarding infertility. Leanne has a compelling voice; I was engaged in her and Ian's journey. The disappointment, difficulties, the rawness with the joy and humour. I highly recommend this book to those who are dealing with infertility and the professionals that are engaged with them."

Carol Comerford
Mental Health Counsellor/Social Worker

This inspirational read, *18 Years in the Making; For This Child We Prayed*, will hold your attention and perhaps renew your faith in dreams cracked open, especially in places of barrenness and infertility, where possibilities were closing their doors.

This story, despite disappointment and deep pain, reveals the quest of love and the seed of faith that God has not forgotten.

Deb White
Senior Minister C3 Monash

"This is such a beautiful book of hope. When God makes a promise, He keeps it. His yes is yes! I still remember the day sitting in church when the announcement was made that Leanne was pregnant, such a roar of celebration and happy tears! When one member of the church celebrates, they all do. I was very blessed to raise my second daughter at the same time as Leanne was raising her son, we have shared a lot of fun memories. Leanne was born to be a mother. I have never met someone else better with children and babies than her. Read the book. It will remind you that God is good."

Narelle Crichton

"I would like to congratulate Leanne on writing her first book. I thoroughly enjoyed reading her story and love how honest she is in telling her family's journey. Going through many years of dreaming of having a child and finally becoming a parent, Leanne shares all the highs and lows along the way. This is a story of hope and love and I know Leanne will help many others by sharing her journey. A well written story that will tug at your heart and leave you feeling such happiness. Congratulations again, Leanne, I look forward to seeing where this journey of becoming an author takes you."

Julie Fisher
Author

Contents

Dedication iii
Testimonials v
Introduction 1
Chapter One: Dreams Cracked, a Love Met 5
Chapter Two: The Rollercoaster Begins 17
Chapter Three: Leave Your Dignity at the Door 25
Chapter Four: Love to Share 35
Chapter Five: New Home; Renewed Faith 45
Chapter Six: New Hope 53
Chapter Seven: Possibly Adoption? 63
Chapter Eight: Secret Hope 69
Chapter Nine: Two Lines 77
Chapter Ten: God Remembered 87
Chapter Eleven: Coming Home 93
Chapter Twelve: Cross Generational Connections 101
Thoughts From Ian 107
About The Author 115
Speaker Bio 119

Introduction

Writing this book has been a journey in itself. It has been a journey of healing and facing the fears of showing strangers some of the most vulnerable moments in my life. Be aware, it is raw in some places, but to tell this story I believe it needed to be.

I had always dreamed of writing a book and allowed the fears of 'what would people think' hold me back. Fear of man is a debilitating place to live in and can stop us from living out of our gifts. That is how it was for me anyway.

It is hard to recall every experience, word, encouragement or disappointment I had over the eighteen years, but I have attempted to retell the journey with the key points and moments that will remain with me forever. My relationships with my family and friends held me in a place of sanity, even when I felt I was going crazy.

My relationship with Jesus is my journey, I am not a minister or a theologian, I only know the experiences I have had with God are very real to me and the scriptures helped me through the many years. I truly believe the pregnancy was a miracle from God, there is no other explanation I have found to explain the successful conception. My hope is that as you read through the journey you will see that hope is available for you too and believe that our God is a good God who wants the best for you. He will walk the hard years with you as I felt He did for me. I am no one special in society, I am not rich or famous, nor am I especially talented in an area that would hold me up for recognition. I am a woman who lives my life as best as I can with my family, dealing with all the circumstances and situations an ordinary life brings and God is still interested in me and loves me. This is my experience.

CHAPTER ONE

Dreams Cracked, a Love Met

Everyone has dreams for their future; some dreams are big, some are small, and some could be thought of as *normal*. I had normal dreams—get a job, get married, and have at least four kids. Not big dreams, just normal ones. Little did I know how hard the dream of being a mother would become.

My parents and older brother were living in the Lower Blue Mountains when I was born in 1968. I was the second born of twin girls, there were six minutes between us, with my sister taking the role of being older very seriously. My younger sister arriving a two and a half years later. We moved as a family in the early 1970s to a mining town in Arnhem Land in the Northern Territory (NT), a place where the air raid sirens left from WWII would sound warnings for everyone to get inside as wild buffalo roamed the streets. It was scary and exciting when this happened, and I always hoped the buffalos would come down our street, but they never did. Although I was still very young, I have great memories of living in the NT. The heat, the build-up to the wet season before the rains came, kids and some adults dancing in the streets, standing under the gutters as they overflowed, getting drenched. Finally, the oppression of the humidity build-up released with the first downpour of the wet season.

We were there when Cyclone Tracy hit Darwin in 1974, it hit our town Christmas night, after it had destroyed Darwin Christmas morning. I remember my parents talking about the cyclone coming and what it had done to Darwin, we spent Christmas Day running around securing everything loose in the yard, Mum setting us all up in the bathroom, it being the strongest room in the house, with blankets, food and water, to spend the night. The sound of the wind howling around the house and torrential rain on the roof, we huddled together hoping the roof would stay on and it did. We were luckier than Darwin as most of the houses in town were made of brick and by the time it hit us the ferocity had weakened. The next day, Boxing Day, most of the men in town headed to Darwin to help with the clean-up there.

My parents' marriage was not the best, although as a child I was unaware of this. My dad wasn't around much as he did shift work as a fireman, and being the 1970s, married women were expected to be at home—working women were rare—Mum stayed at home to raise us. My parents separated and we moved back to the Blue Mountains, with Dad staying in the NT. I remember not being concerned that Dad didn't come back with us; as I said, he wasn't around that much and we were told he had stayed for work. When my parents divorced, I was seven, nearly eight, it was horrible, I didn't understand what was happening and as most kids from broken homes do, I felt it must have been my fault in some way. It was years before I saw Dad again.

Mum and us kids moved again, this time to the Central Coast in New South Wales (NSW), a couple of hours north of Sydney. Our new home was in a little three street coastal village, with a beach and corner shop. The trip to town took about an hour and the primary school we attended was very small, only three classrooms with years four, five and six in the one room. We were the only kids in school whose parents were divorced and as you could imagine, this led to a lot of teasing. This was where we were living when I started high school.

I was fifteen the first time I was told having kids might be a problem.

Mum and I were sitting in the doctor's office, after years of debilitating periods that would send me to bed for a week, being told there was a great chance I would never be able to have children. I was fifteen years old! The news rocked me to the core, and I thought to myself, *are you kidding me? This can't be right. I'm too young to be told something like this. It doesn't make sense at all.*

I was the sort of person who loved kids. You know, one of those annoyingly baby obsessed people. I would go to a party and everybody else would be hanging out together playing and whatever. But there was me, in the back yard playing with the toddlers. I never saw not being able to have children as a part of my life. It was a huge shock for me and for my family. There is not a lot you could do with information like that, especially when you are fifteen. I pretty much convinced myself the doctor was wrong; *how could he know that when I'm so young?* I wondered. How could I believe this diagnosis? I convinced myself things could and would change. *Things will change when I'm ready to start a family, I may grow out of whatever is going on in my body. Medicine will change and whatever the problem is, it will be an easy fix.*

I continued with school until an opportunity to do my Enrolled Nursing training in the hospital system presented itself. I left school six weeks into Year 12 and moved from the little coastal village to the big smoke of Sydney. Registered Nursing training had not long transferred into the university system and I didn't want to go there. It was 1986, I was seventeen, moving into the nurse's accommodation attached to the training hospital on Sydney's North Shore, leaving my family and friends. I was now out on my own. I didn't know anyone in Sydney, but the accommodation was full of trainees in the same position as me, so we connected and bonded quickly, looking out for each other.

After completing my training and spending five years in Sydney, it was time to move on. I went to the South Coast in NSW to continue my studies, finally feeling ready to go to university. That was where I met the love of my life...in a snooker room.

I was never like most girls my age; I wasn't into clothes, or makeup, or movie stars. I loved going to the pub and shooting pool and hanging out with the boys. While I may not of have been the only girl there, I was the only female there serious about playing the game. I loved it.

I ran the pool competition at the local pub that had a first prize of $1000 up for grabs, I had won it a couple of times. One day a group of snooker players came in and took it out, wiping the floor with the local players. They invited me to come try the *real* game, so off I went to the local RSL to have a go at snooker. I arrived early and was one of the first people there. The boys all started trickling in and seeing a girl in there, which wasn't a common occurrence, one by one came and sat next to me to have a little chat. One of them was this tall, giant of a man, he comes in and sits down next to me, asking lots of questions. Little did I know at the time, he would be my future husband.

But Ian knew. When he walked into the room and saw me, a thought ran through his head, *there's the girl I'm going to marry*. That was why he came and sat next to me and started chatting. He told me this after I had accepted his proposal and is a story we love to retell.

It took a while for me to agree to go out with him. Ian started coming to the pool competitions and I was going to snooker so we were seeing each other twice a week and became friends, I eventually agreed to go on a date and Ian spoilt me rotten. He fed me lobster and took me dancing and when he brought me home we sat for hours, just talking. He didn't even try to hold my hand. Wow. It was after that night I realised this guy was too good for me and told him we could only be friends. I had a very low self-esteem at the time and I'd had a few relationships that didn't work out, confirming to myself that I wasn't worth a good relationship. Ian was the *boy next door*; shy and respectful. Funny thing though, I never realised he was shy until I saw him with my friends whom he didn't know, he had always been very animated with me.

Ian would ask me out again periodically and couldn't understand why I wouldn't go out with him. In my own stupid way I was trying to protect him from me—my sense of unworthiness was ruling my emotions.

I decided to go on holidays with my twin sister and we drove to the Northern Territory from the South Coast in NSW, which was roughly a seven-day drive, that took us ten, as we stayed in Townsville for three days to visit friends, before driving west into the NT. Although I wanted to just be friends with Ian, he was still keen for a relationship. He agreed to stay in my flat, as I didn't want to give it up while I was away and as he still lived at home with his family, he didn't have his own place to look after and was happy to help. One afternoon, about a week after I left, the police came around to my place looking for me, a Jane Doe had been found in Sydney and couldn't be identified. Her picture was in all the papers and on the news, someone had rung in identifying that it was me. I was also driving through Sydney around the time of her discovery. This was the early 1990s before mobile phones were commonplace so there was no way Ian could make contact. Ian called the place I was going to so he could let me know I needed to head to the police station and verify that I was alive. It was a hard and confusing situation, but he sorted it out as best he could.

This whole scenario showed me Ian was dependable and able to sort things out without overreacting or running away because things looked or got too hard and complicated.

After a month of being away I returned from my holiday. Ian wasn't there when I arrived home. I was having a cup of tea on the lounge when the door opened and Ian came into the flat with the biggest bunch of flowers I had ever seen. I took one look at him and felt a huge reaction in my body; my stomach jumped and I started blushing, I realised this was the bloke for me but did he still want to go out with me because I had friend-zoned him so often? I jumped up and ran to give him a hug, I was excited to see him and with a nervous smile on my face I asked him if the flowers were for me. Ian just looked me straight in the eyes and said plainly, with no anger, "No." My heart sank, *yep, I've blown it*, I thought. Ian then explained they *were* going to be for me. Ian had planned to come home and clean the flat, putting the flowers around as a surprise but he decided not to give them to me because of my selfish behaviour. I hadn't let him know when I would be home or communicated my returning plans with him in any way, so no, the flowers were not for me.

As silly as it sounds, this was the sentence confirming Ian was the man for me. Not afraid to express how he was really feeling, no fear of losing my friendship by chipping my behaviour. Yes, this was the type of relationship I wanted. It was real. I needed to know if he was still interested in going out, so I asked him. When he said yes, I felt relief and excitement for our possible future. Ian was like no one I had ever gone out with before. He treated me as someone who mattered, someone precious. To find our love together when we were both twenty-two was a blessing.

He was—and still is—calm, dependable, and whenever I was with him I always felt so safe and the best thing was the way he always made me laugh with his keen sense of irony and dry humour. Ian could turn my anxiety and stress around and help me see situations from a different perspective. He is still all these things to me; he is a good man.

The whirlwind romance had begun! We had been going out for about three months when we went to a party. There were a few families there with little babies and one was a little boy named Ian. Being the child crazed, baby obsessed person that I was, I was having the best time getting baby cuddles. I walked over to Ian with the baby and asked if he would like to have a hold of his namesake.

And he said, "No, no I don't want to."

I was shocked at his response, so I pushed it. "Come on, hold the baby."

"I don't want to," he said.

I start getting upset, freaking out and thinking to myself, *I've finally found this fantastic bloke and he doesn't like kids! How is this even possible? How could he not like kids!* My mind was in a spin, stressing. I explained how I was feeling and really needed to know why he didn't want to hold the baby?

Ian put his arm around me and he looked me straight in my eyes. He said, "You know Leanne, I've never held a baby before. And I want the first baby I hold to be my own."

Relief swept over me, and I thought, *okay that's a reasonable answer, crisis averted, he's still a good bloke.* I gave the baby back to his mum and we continued having a great night together.

On the way home from the party, we were crossing the Sydney Harbour Bridge and I was talking about the baby and how I thought it was a lovely thing that he wanted the first baby he held to be his own. Then he said, "And I want it to be yours, too."

I was gobsmacked and wondered if Ian just proposed to me. Was that what just happened? Yes, yes it was. It was April 1992 and we had been going out for only three months when this happened. Those were the words he used to propose and I replied, "I would love that too."

Our families were over the moon for us. Ian's mum ran to her room and came out with a box that had various rings and other pieces of jewellery. It had belonged to her mum, Ian's grandmother and asked me if I would like to choose a ring. I chose a beautiful, fire opal that Ian's grandfather had given his wife when they were on a trip to Lightening Ridge.

The wedding plans began with the date being set for February the following year. Ian took me out to dinner one night, about three months after the Harbour Bridge proposal, to a restaurant which had glorious views of the coastline. We ordered a seafood platter for two, there was a pianist playing and a dance floor. It was so romantic. We had already agreed on the Anne Murray song 'Could I Have This Dance for the Rest of My Life' as our wedding waltz and when the pianist started playing it, I got excited and wanted to dance. Ian was not that keen but agreed anyway and as we were dancing, in the middle of the song, in the middle of the dance floor, Ian got down on one knee and formally proposed! It was the first time he had actually used the words *will you marry me*. Being an emotional woman, my eyes welled with happy tears and nodded my head *yes* as the whole restaurant cheered. That was why he hadn't been keen to dance; Ian had requested the song and planned on proposing at the table.

We were married in February 1993 when we were both twenty-four.

DREAMS CRACKED, A LOVE MET

CHAPTER TWO

The Rollercoaster Begins

I had explained to Ian before we were married that we might have problems having kids so the decision was made we would start trying straight away—we actually started trying about three months before we got married.

Beginning our lives together was exciting, we built our first home to *lockup stage* and enjoyed our first year together settling into the new community we had moved to. It can normally take up to a year to fall pregnant so after twelve months we decided to go the doctor and have some tests done to find out if there were any real problems and if so, what they were and what we could do about them.

Our test results came back. Ian was an extremely fertile man, there were no issues with him. I, on the other hand, had two issues identified; Endometriosis, which was the reason for all the pains and the cramps, inhibiting the fertilised egg attaching to the wall of the uterus and probably the reason my family doctor told me at fifteen I would have trouble conceiving. The doctor had probably explained this to Mum but this was the first time it had been explained to me and given a name. The second condition was polycystic ovary syndrome (POCS) which meant that I didn't ovulate regularly. There were a lot of other symptoms attached to these conditions, but these are the ones that had the greatest impact on my fertility.

The series of tests that were run went for months, with early morning blood tests and they showed that on average I ovulated about once a year. The first treatment prescribed was fertility drugs which should increase my chances of ovulation. The doctor suggested we try IVF straight away, but I wasn't ready for that. At that time, it had been only eight years since the first successful IVF baby had been born in Australia, and it was incredibly expensive; tens of thousands of dollars expensive. The general consensus was that IVF was for older women wanting to have children, not for someone in their early to mid-twenties. I was not keen to be going to do IVF with women in their 40s, I truly believed I would not need to go down that path anyway.

When we started the treatment I weighed around sixty kilograms. At the time, I did not have a lot of hormonal activity in my body and taking these drugs increased that,

THE ROLLERCOASTER BEGINS

so my body went crazy. I started putting on weight; twenty kilograms in six weeks. *Yes,* you read that right!

So, there I was, unable to conceive and wearing all my husband's clothes because none of my clothes fit me anymore. I felt as though my whole identity was disappearing. The idea I had in my head about what it was to be a woman and who I was turning out to be as a woman, were not adding up. *It shouldn't be like this! Woman are supposed to be able to have babies.* It was a reality I had never seen before, none of my friends or family had this problem, I had no point of reference for how I was feeling or what was going on, I was feeling very alone.

Family were having kids, our friends were having kids. New life was popping up all around me and while I was excited about this on one hand, an intense sense of jealously was taking over on the other hand. I didn't like feeling that way, this wasn't me. But I couldn't work out *why not me*? It was not that I didn't want others to be having children, I just wanted it to be me as well. A dream that our kids could grow up together and be there for each other, was slipping away with each passing year.

I was fighting an internal battle that no one else could see. Who was this person looking back at me in the mirror? I didn't recognise her; I didn't realise that that's what constant disappointment could do to you. Where had my happiness gone? My fun-loving attitude to life was not there anymore. No one could see the internal battle, but they could see the repercussions of it. The tears, the disbelief and the frustrations. I separated my emotions and my life. I went to parties, work, BBQs, and as long as no one mentioned kids or asked me how I was going with the fertility treatment, I was okay. I could hold my emotions in check. It didn't take much to expose my pain though; one question about the treatment or meeting new people and being asked how many kids I had, and the pain bubbled to the surface, usually by leaking out my eyes.

It was now three years since we had started our journey to parenthood, I was still on the fertility drugs and taking my temperature every morning to check if I was ovulating. I remember Ian telling me that he woke up in the middle of the night to find me asleep with the thermometer in my mouth! There were charts to fill out and documenting of moments of intimacy and if there was one thing I learnt from all of this was that nothing destroys the joy of lovemaking more than the infertility road. Everything gets allocated; times best to be intimate with the greatest chance for successful conception. Removing all romance and spontaneity. It had now become a clinical operation.

It was 1996 and I was fully convinced that I was finally pregnant, which wasn't unusual because when you are trying to have kids, you can convince yourself that you are pregnant every single month. I went to my doctor for a test which showed that I was! I raced off to get a blood test to confirm and the results came the next day. My heart stopped. I was pregnant, finally, it was true! It was a Friday, and I remember it like it was yesterday. It was the most amazing feeling. Finally, our dreams were on their way to becoming a reality. Three years trying to fall pregnant—the angst, the frustration, and the disappointments—was finally over. All my fears disappeared, Ian came home with a giant bunch of flowers and we celebrated together. There was so much love and joy and laughter in the house. We rang all our family to spread the news. It was one of the best weekends of our life to that point.

Then Monday came around and I started miscarrying. To have everything reverse so quickly was heartbreaking. The joy turned to sorrow and grief. We were devastated. I had never felt grief like it before. I got up in the middle of the night and wailed and wailed. I had never cried so hard in my life before. I was screaming out the pain, screaming out the distress. There were no words, just grief. By the time I finished crying I felt like the biggest weight had been lifted from my heart, I was only left with sadness.

Ian lay in bed listening not knowing what to do, he couldn't fix it.

Then came the phone calls to let everyone know.

It took two weeks to miscarry, the doctors wanted to let nature take its course.

It was after this point I wanted to release Ian from his promise to me. It was not fair on him that he may never have kids if he stayed with me, but if he found someone new he could be a dad. I'll never forget his response.

"You are not infertile on your own Leanne; we are infertile together. I didn't marry you so I could be a dad. Remember that."

I needed to learn how to deal with my disappointments and grief. The hospital where I was working had counselling available, so I booked myself in. The first couple of sessions went well until one of the other staff members, who worked on a different ward and whom I did not know well, asked me how the counselling was going. She was also seeing the counsellor, and confidentiality had been broken as they discussed my issues with each other. I knew this as she asked me about personal details I had only shared in my session. I felt betrayed and vulnerable not knowing if my details had been shared with others, I stopped going to the hospital counsellor after that, I couldn't trust her.

That was one of the big things I learnt about counselling; it is so important you find someone you connect with, find the perfect counsellor for you. While you may need to see a few before you find a good fit for your personality and your issues, that is okay. Don't give up on the counselling route because the first counsellor didn't work out for you.

CHAPTER THREE

Leave Your Dignity at the Door

After the miscarriage, we were hoping that my body now knew what to do, and it wouldn't be long before I fell pregnant again. It wasn't quite a year of not falling pregnant before we looked into seeing an IVF specialist, as my body really had no idea what to do.

We were back on the rollercoaster of blood tests, hospital procedures, a couple of operations and lots more tests in general. It was *again* discovered that Ian is extremely fertile, and I was not. My test results not only showed I was not fertile, but another condition on top of the endometriosis and the POCS had been discovered. I had a hostile womb as well; where the womb environment kills off the sperm before it can fertilise the egg. I won't go into the test that discovers that condition because it was the most horrifically, embarrassing test I ever had to endure. If you have had the test, you know what I mean.

It wasn't just medical changes we made to our lives, during the whole process I changed the way I ate. I have never drunk coffee, only tea, so I changed to herbal, caffeine free teas. I even got into Kombucha, trying to fix the acidity in my body. I went to herbalists and nutritionists, stopped drinking alcohol and exercised, but the weight still came on due to the hormone treatment; there were no changes in any of the conditions that were stopping me from getting pregnant. So many well-meaning people informed me that I could change the acidity levels in my body that caused the hostile womb condition by what I was eating; changing my diet didn't change anything.

The clinic we were attending had a support group for us all, which I was very excited about going to. There were about eight couples including us and I was looking forward to being able to talk with others in the same position as Ian and myself, knowing and understanding how we were feeling. I wanted to express all my fears; my fears of failure, my fears of never becoming a mum. Unfortunately, the group wasn't controlled very well.

There was one woman who constantly took over, rarely giving anyone else a chance to speak and she made a statement. "I know that everybody here is going to fall pregnant and we're not going to talk about it not working."

This statement completely shut all the couples down, nobody felt comfortable in sharing their fears of failure or sharing how it was affecting them, their marriage, or life in general. This was evident with the silence that filled the room after her statement. After attending the group a few times with the same atmosphere, Ian and I felt unable to express ourselves, we felt it wasn't helping us, so we stopped going.

For young women—especially myself—there is an assumption that everybody can fall pregnant. Growing up, in school we were told *don't have sex, you'll get pregnant.* There was very little conversation on infertility, if any at all, so it can be quite a shock to the system when you start trying and you're not pregnant after the first month, then you're not pregnant after the third month, and then one year has passed and the next thing you know you are on the rollercoaster of fertility treatment...at least this was how it was for me.

Infertility is very much a silent problem, although since the first successful IVF baby in Australia in 1980 the conversation in society has increased. In the early 1990s the success rate for IVF was very low. Even today, the success rate is below 39% for women aged between eighteen and thirty-four, and the rate drops even more the older you get.

Older women experiencing infertility were often discussed in the media, it was a popular subject on morning television and talk shows since IVF had now become a possibility, with the basic solution being, "Don't wait until you're too old to have kids, but if you do wait and have trouble conceiving, at least there's IVF now." It was rare for the low success rates to be discussed or the effects the treatment had on women; I thought these reports were presented more like a fairy-tale solution for older women. The media presentations showed little understanding of the real concerns or problems being faced by infertile couples. One particular husband spoke with us about the shock he felt when IVF failed for them and his disbelief as the procedures had been presented to them as a solution and not a possibility.

Young women, on the other hand, with problems conceiving are rarely, if ever, discussed in the media. I never saw any media coverage on young couples experiencing infertility. The feelings of separation from society with what we were going through increased, I felt infertility in young couples was still a taboo subject.

When talking with new work mates or people I had just met, and the 'get to know you' questions were asked, "Are you married?" "How many kids do you have?" I wouldn't always answer with infertility straight away but the answer of "no kids yet" would inevitably lead to the next question being, "When are you planning on kids?" "Don't wait too long!" When I would answer, "I can't have kids," there was always a specific set of reactions. The conversation topic was changed, which was okay, or more often the common comments and questions would come out:

"Are you really infertile?"

"What are you worried about? You're still young, you have plenty of time."

"You're thinking too much, stop thinking about it and it will happen."

"Go on a holiday."

"Start a new job."

And my personal favourite; "You're trying too hard."

I found these statements to be blaming, putting the responsibility of the lack of conception onto the couple themselves. Even to this day I would like to know *how*; how can you try too hard? The answer still eludes me. It is like blaming someone if they get arthritis or go blind; it is their own fault, their incorrect attitude or thought process that created the problem. Which of course we know to be incorrect. Statements like these also shuts conversations down, which in all fairness is better, as you can't talk to people if they have no real understanding or desire to understand the issue. Often the subject of infertility is too uncomfortable for them.

It was 1997 and we were preparing to start IVF. I had to give myself an injection at the same time of day, every day for a month, but I couldn't do it. I sat for what felt like hours with the needle in my hand, but I was frozen. I just couldn't stab myself. I rang one of my best friends, who I had worked with at the hospital and was a great support to me with all that we had gone through to get to this point. She was, as most nurses are, comforting, supportive and realistic about the process we were beginning. Ian and I went over to her place. There was a real sense of excitement as we talked about what this would mean to our lives if it actually worked. Our anticipation was high as we began the next phase to family. Ian took over the injections the next day after practising on an orange before having a go on me! Not bad for a cabinet maker.

Infertility treatments and IVF are not a pretty or romantic way to conceive; my body was on the receiving end of a barrage of treatments. There were hormone injections, *more* weight gain, early morning trips to pathology for blood tests, external and internal ultrasounds and hospital procedures under general anaesthetic. There was a lot of stress, a lot of hope, a lot of dashing of hopes when test results were not positive, a lot of emotional outbreaks and outbursts and so many tears; I didn't realise anyone could cry so much. I felt like I was on an emotional rollercoaster all the time, yoyoing up to anger and down to depression, but all the time in a constant state of frustration. One of the other side effects of all these extra hormones screaming through my body was hot flushes. Hot Flushes! I wasn't even thirty yet and I was having hot flushes! The first time it happened we were with family playing a board game on the loungeroom floor, it was winter and I was wearing UGG boots. Suddenly I was hot, boiling hot, I broke out in a sweat and felt like I was on fire. I started ripping my boots and jumper off and almost took my shirt off in an attempt to cool down, then I realised everyone was yelling at me, asking what was happening! Thank goodness they did, I could have ended up naked! When the heat was taking over my body it was like the room had disappeared, leaving me unaware of anything other than the heat coursing through my body! The following hot flushes I experienced were never as bad as that first one.

I went in for the harvesting. They got sixteen eggs altogether with only nine being viable, so although it was not the best result it certainly was not the worst. My heart broke for one of the women who was going through the treatment at the same time as us, who didn't end up having any eggs to collect. Donor eggs were not readily available in 1997.

We had so much support from our families walking this journey with us, we were blessed to have them being there and loving us. My mother-in-law and sister-in-law were there for us on the ground, living not far from us and we were so grateful for their love and support; it would have been hard without them. My mum and twin sister lived over 1700-kilometres away, while my brother was travelling Australia and my younger sister was overseas. The number of times I rang Mum or my twin sister and all they heard were tears on the other end were countless. Ian and I were lucky to have so many in our corner hoping for successful treatment for us.

It was nearing the end of 1997 and we were about to do the last full round of IVF, Ian had to go overseas for work. He left a couple of days before the procedure, so my mother-in-law came in with me for the implanting of the embryos and the thought of this being successful while Ian was out of the country was incredible! We were laughing together at the thought of this being the best conception/birth story ever! It is a lovely memory I cherish.

The three rounds of IVF were unsuccessful, and finances were tight; we couldn't afford another round in the near future. We hadn't given up hope though as the specialist was trialling a new procedure that had some success overseas. It was a form of artificial insemination, but after three unsuccessful attempts of that we decided it was enough for the time being. We stopped the medical intervention in 1998, our marriage was getting strained with the full focus being on pregnancy, our finances were in dire straits and the emotional turmoil was taking its toll.

At the same time we were doing the IVF, I decided I needed God but didn't want to go to a traditional church. I had been in a traditional church when I was younger and had been confirmed when I was twelve. I was roughly fourteen when the minister was asking if anyone wanted to be an altar boy. I offered, but the minister said *no*; he didn't want two angels with him on a Sunday. I explained to him my twin sister didn't want to do it, it was just me, but he still said no, he ended up with no one. I could only think it was because I was a girl. I stopped going to church after that as I didn't want to be going anywhere that wouldn't have girls around or allow them a voice. I remembered that rejection and I wasn't willing to set myself up for that again, so I found a spiritual church to go to.

I learnt about crystal healings and began tarot reading, I attended lots of spiritual healing circles looking for the answer and healing. At one particular meeting, the medium running the night said we could ask her one question, only one and we would be told the truth. I was excited. *I'm finally going to get my answer*, I thought.

It was my turn. "When am I going to have a child?" I asked confident of a positive response.

"Never," she said, moving on like she told me I wouldn't be getting any pizza tonight.

I felt like I had just been slapped in the face. It felt like a cold and callous lie and when I reacted in distress by bursting into tears, the look on her face was disbelief. There was no understanding from her how this statement could have upset me. It was nothing to her but everything to me. My desire for a child was still there, I couldn't accept what I had been told. *When is someone going to understand where I'm coming from and give me hope that I would one day be a mum?* I thought. My heart was broken but I was still not ready to accept the reality I was living in, I was still searching for the answer and determined to find it. Although I continued with tarot reading, I stopped going to the healing circles, I was not willing to accept the answers they had for me.

CHAPTER FOUR

Love to Share

New Year's Eve 1997 arrived and I was turning thirty that coming year. I had always been a real 'go get them' sort of girl and felt that since our wedding we had been in a holding pattern, waiting for the next phase of our life to start. It felt like a lifetime of grief in our road to parenthood. Although at this time we were still having IVF treatment, I had this massive revelation it was time to stop thinking about ourselves and what we couldn't have, it was time to think about the next step. What did we have that we could help others with? We had a house with empty rooms that we could fill with kids. We could foster.

Ian and I had already talked about fostering children before we were married. The plan had been that we would have our own kids and wait until they grew up a bit and then we would foster. We could give a good life to kids that were not as fortunate, needing a family and stability. Both of us had life experiences that were not perfect, apart from the experiences of our own journey together. We were aware of the condition these children could arrive in and the possible life experiences they may have had.

It was the end of 1998, a couple of months after our last failed attempt of IVF, that Ian and I discussed fostering again and agreed we wouldn't wait any longer. We researched the procedure to become foster parents and signed up for the training. I felt that I had purpose again, although I was still hopeful of having our own baby, my mind wasn't completely focused on it anymore. Joy had come back into our lives as we set ourselves up for this new venture.

I was still working as a nurse at that time on the ward at the local hospital and decided to go on casual so I would have more availability if a child needed to come into the foster care system. We completed the training through the Department of Child Services, DOCS. This was before other agencies were involved in fostering to a great extent. We signed up for long-term fostering, which means we would be happy to take the child or children until they were eighteen. *Due to the privacy laws, I will not be giving any information that could possibly identify the children we fostered.

Two days after the completion of the training in April 1999, we got a call there was a two-week-old baby in neonatal ICU that needed a foster home. The child was drug affected and required morphine to help withdraw from the drugs that were in the child's system—we had been chosen because of my medical experience. They were hoping we could pick up the baby in three days.

"Three days! Yes, of course we'll take the munchkin." So, I spent the next three days running around like a mad chook with its head cut off, as you do, trying to get my house sorted for this new baby. I visited friends who had not long had a child to find out exactly what was needed. Start off with six singlets, six onesies, bottles, formula, a cot, a pram and a car seat, and not to forget the cloth nappies. Disposable nappies were around then but they were incredibly expensive.

Ian was as excited as I was. The day I went to pick the baby up was full of anticipation and a little bit of fear. Most people have months to prepare themselves for looking after a newborn, we only had three days. At least I had my years of baby obsession and my nursing training behind me. The caseworker met me at the neonatal ICU and the tiny two-week-old baby was put in my arms. This baby was so little, 00000 sized clothes were too big. Michael (name has been changed) slept all the way home. Though there was not much sleeping after that.

For the next six weeks every waking hour was filled with withdrawal cries that only settled after medication. Michael needed lots of love and as little amount of handling as possible. Withdrawing from drugs makes their little bodies hypersensitive and it can be painful to touch or hold them too much. It was a stressful time knowing the importance of touch to a newborn. It was a real balancing act, but as the withdrawals lessened the cuddles increased.

Ian and I were very aware that Michael could be moved on at any time, so we protected our hearts as best we could. Taking it one week at a time and talking about our feelings as much as possible. That was until the day the caseworker assigned to Michael's case stated there was a great chance we would have this child until he turned eighteen. She couldn't see the possibility of the birth mother regaining custody as the circumstances of the birth family was not getting any better and he was not the only child of hers in care.

It was this statement that changed our way of thinking about fostering; it again became about us and the possibility of our own family. We began to dream, hoping that we could eventually adopt this child and our hearts opened to falling completely in love. We thought it was safe. Michael was meeting milestones and starting to thrive. When Michael was close to six months old the birth mother changed her circumstances and the birth father had been sent to prison, she started seeing the child on a more regular basis.

In all honesty my heart broke for her, I couldn't imagine what she was going through, losing her baby into foster care and I suppose I was naïve, but after a few months when I would go to her place to do drop off and pickup for her visits, I started staying back and helping her, giving her confidence in caring for Michael. I also needed to know that he was going to be safe.

The birth mum was improving and the birth father was out of the picture. It was at this point I knew she was going to regain custody and we would have to say goodbye. I prayed,

"God, if we aren't going to be this child's parents, we just want to see Michael walking, talking and healthy."

At ten months old the laws had changed, allowing the mother to regain custody although she was still on the methadone program, a program offered to help people get off harder drugs. The decision from DOCS was made; the birth mum would regain custody. The transition from our house to the new house was done well, with as less stress on Michael as possible. It went over six weeks, spending an extra night per week at his new home until it was time for the permanent move. DOCS collected him from our home and that was the hardest day of our lives. Our hearts were broken, but we wanted to be excited for him, hoping they would have a good life together. And that was—still is—the way I like to think about it as I cannot allow myself to think otherwise. I had allowed myself to believe that Michael would join our family permanently, I needed to believe that him returning to his mother was the right choice from DOCS and he would be okay.

Two weeks later, DOCS asked if we would have Michael every second weekend, his mum was not coping as well as was expected and with not enough thought into our own mental health we readily agreed. This arrangement continued until Michael was fifteen months old, when he was walking, talking in short sentences and healthy.

Ian and I decided we would continue fostering. The next child arrived within weeks of Michael leaving and was in primary school—we'll call him John for privacy—and he had a horrendous background story. John needed to be in a house with no other children and as Michael was only there for two weekends in the month DOCS felt that we were a good match for John. He was only allowed at school for three to five hours a week. DOCS supplied us with a behavioural specialist who would come out to help engage John and strategize the best ways for caring for him. John had minimal contact with his family and would only see them a couple of times a month. It was a difficult situation for all of us. John craved male attention and disregarded females as he had always been around women but had very little respect for them. Many of John's carers, outside of the foster system, had drug and alcohol problems themselves and were in and out of jail. We were his first permanent fosters parents, having not long been in the system. We had to take baby steps to build a level of trust with him.

One hot day early in summer when Ian was at work, I took John to the beach. We went with some friends whose kids were around the same age as John. They didn't know the area well so followed us to the rock pool in their car. We were having a great day and after being there a few hours it was time to go. John was not keen to leave and climbed a tree near the cars, refusing to come down. After nearly an hour of lots of coaxing and even an attempt from me to climb the tree—which only made John climb higher and me worry that the branch would break—we had no luck in getting him to come down. Our friends thought that they would drive around the corner out of sight while I stayed to encourage him out of the tree. We hoped without an audience he would come down, and that is exactly what happened. Once we got into the car and headed around the corner, our friends started following us. When John saw the other car following he completely lost his temper, the betrayal he felt over being tricked was heartbreaking to watch.

John was very smart, although he tried to hide it from everyone. We were told he couldn't read and or understand maths, although in Grade five John was thought to be at a first grade level. We soon discovered he was very smart. He loved to play chess with Ian and would wait every afternoon for him to come home from work so they could play. One day in the supermarket I saw John reading the label of a bag that had a rope in it. "Clothesline," he said. If he couldn't read, he would have said rope.

At the time, my mum was visiting and we would play scrabble together. John didn't want to play but loved to watch. That afternoon Mum and I set up the scrabble board to play, with John sitting next to Mum as usual. I relayed to Mum the story of what I saw in the supermarket and how I thought John really could read. I told the story as if he was not sitting next to her. John argued with me, saying there had been a picture of a clothesline on the label. I didn't look at John when I said to Mum, "And the strangest thing was, there wasn't even a picture to tell John what the rope was for." John jumped up and hugged me for the briefest moment as if to say 'thank you for seeing me' and then ran off to the lounge room where he sat in front of the TV, his little body shaking in fear because, I assumed, he had let his guard down. It was horrible to see him react this way but also encouraging as we were starting to break down some of his barriers.

John had been with us for a little over three months and it was nearing the end of the school year when John was coerced to run away by members of his family and was subsequentially hidden by them. The story broke on the news programs and caused quite an uproar. We were frustrated as we were not allowed to speak to the media or be involved in any way to find John or bring him home. The media reports inflamed the situation and very little truth was shared. John was released from the foster care system back to his family, we assumed due to the negative media reports. Ian and I were exhausted and our hearts were broken again. We decided that we couldn't foster anymore; we both needed a break and time to recover and heal. I have felt that I failed John in many ways and wished for a better result for him, although many of our friends and family felt that the foster system failed the kids as well as us.

CHAPTER FIVE

New Home; Renewed Faith

Nothing in the world comes easy, everything has trials or burdens attached at some point. There are those that can conceive easily but other areas of their life may be hard. Sometimes we just want to leave it all behind and move away from the stress and hardship to start again.

I was overwhelmed with feelings of failure, failing at conceiving, failing at IVF and failing at fostering. Would my *normal* dream of being a mum ever eventuate? Ian and I weren't doing that great either. We were fighting a lot, finances were tight due to the previous expenses of IVF—although we were both working, every spare cent had been funnelled into what had now become a black hole. We were both so disappointed in how our life was turning out. We couldn't change our circumstances by saying, "Yes, we'll have a baby now." And we were not willing to give up on our dream of having a family of our own.

It was early 2000, we had been married for seven years at this point, but there was very little romance left. There was so much pressure on our relationship with my intense need to have a child. It consumed me to the point that Ian did not feel he was able to express his own grief over the whole situation...he stopped talking. Generally, men find it hard to communicate their problems for the sake of just talking about it. Men like to be able to fix things and this was something Ian could not fix no matter how hard he tried. Losing our foster baby is a pain that is still with us today. We had been given hope and assurances that Michael would be part of our family until he was eighteen, then to have him removed, broke us and our families as well.

After John had gone, I needed to get away for a holiday and Ian was keen to stay at home, so off I headed to far north Queensland to spend some time with family for two weeks. It was a wonderful time of de-stressing, not having to worry about treatments, or babies, or the fact that I still wasn't pregnant. Just time to be me. Ian and I spoke just about every night, and he was also enjoying his time; giving his head time to clear and concentrate on his own thing.

Ian had been working as a cabinet maker for a local boat building company, doing the internal fit outs for yachts and catamarans. A new job opportunity came up for him whilst I was away and he decided to take it. He called to let me know.

"Hey hun, I quit my job today, but don't worry I'll be starting a new job on Monday," Ian tells me, matter-of-factly.

"Oh okay, where is the new job?" I asked, not expecting the reply I got.

"Far northern New South Wales, near the border of Queensland. I'm leaving this weekend and I'll find a house for us."

It meant moving over one-thousand kilometres away.

I was excited about doing something new and moving didn't stress me out as I was used to moving—we had done it a lot growing up. However, I was sad to leave my friends and family but happy for a new start. Ian was the homebody of the two of us, so for him to have initiated this I knew it was something he needed to do for himself.

I got home from my holiday to an empty house, with Ian not there, excited at the prospect of a new start. I put my notice in at work and started packing up our life. Ian found a place for us and our two dogs to live, so three weeks later he flew home so we could do the nearly twelve-hour drive together. We stopped in to say our final goodbyes to Michael on the way out of town. He was fifteen months old when we moved and haven't seen him since.

We were in a brand-new town a thousand kilometres away from home, from family, from friends, and nobody knew our story. A new beginning for us. It was a refreshing feeling and at the time we did not feel we were running away from our problems; it was more the need to take the pressure off. We had spent eight years in a relatively small town, feeling like everyone knew our story. I would get asked by strangers or acquaintances when I was out grocery shopping if I was pregnant yet. The fertility drugs had given me a lovely pot belly and on more than one occasion I had people congratulating me and asking when I was due! I felt watched and monitored, although in reality, this wasn't the case, that was sometimes how it felt in a small, country town.

Two years prior to moving, I suffered a back injury at work and went into community nursing as there was very little need to lift patients or put any strain on my back. I could not do the intense work on the wards anymore. Community nursing jobs were as rare as hen's teeth, and when we moved I found it difficult to get a job in that area, so I changed vocation, going into office administration.

We had only been in the area for about six weeks when my sister came for a visit. She had been attending Bible college in Sydney and the students came up to the area for a week. She showed me the timetable of all the activities that were planned for each day and asked me to come along. I chose a women's pancake breakfast at the local church because seriously, who doesn't love pancakes! I remember sitting there listening to the message after the breakfast, and the speaker was talking about being bold in life, seeing opportunities and taking them.

This was a whole new experience for me, I had never seen a woman giving a message from the pulpit before and the message was about being bold. That was a first, my previous experiences in church had been about woman being obedient to men and not saying or doing anything without permission. It was also not like the spiritual church I had gone to either, where there was no real foundation or set belief system, whatever you felt at that moment, you went with.

The service finished and a few women came and introduced themselves. I hadn't really met anyone in the area yet, so it was great to chat with some new people. As we were talking my sister came up and asked if she could pray for me with some of the students.

"Yes, yes, of course you can," I said, thinking she would pray for me with her friends someplace else and I would just reap the benefits.

About six girls came back into the room where I was, stood around me and started praying. I felt my whole-body wash over with a feeling of warmth, acceptance and love. I had never felt anything like this before, the sense that I had come home was overwhelming. This was what I had been searching for, it was the realest experience I had ever had in a church. It was in that moment I re-dedicated my life to God.

I started attending church on a regular basis after that, always sitting in the second row, partly so I could be sure God knew I was there, and partly because if I sat at the back

I might be asked to leave...you know...if they knew who I was. I was convinced I would be judged, my experiences told me I would be judged. I thought it was best if I let the minister know who I was, so if they wanted to throw me out, they could. I was pretty convinced a religious organisation would not care to have me around with my experiences with crystal healings, mediums and my tarot reading. And the rejection from when I was fourteen because I was a girl still played through my mind. I was ready for them to ask me to leave because I was convinced nobody wanted those sorts of people in church. But the roof didn't cave in, and I wasn't consumed in fire or covered in coal when I entered the building, so maybe it would be all right.

The response I got was so surprising; there were no lectures or guilt trips, all I got was acceptance and love. I was told that God was not after perfection; come as you are, have an open heart and mind to His word and He will do the rest. *Well, okay then, that is what I will do*, I thought.

A couple of weeks later, one of the girls from the office at church came up to me with a package from Sydney, it was a book titled *God's Plan for Pregnancy: From Conception to Childbirth and Beyond, by Nerida Walker*. I thought, *what is this? Who sent it?* I was excited but a little freaked out because inside the book was a message from one of the students who had prayed for me saying she felt God ask her to send this to me. I thought, *God knows me? He knows my heart's desire and what I want for my life?* I was completely blown away by the fact that this person had sent me this book.

I took this as a *yes* to me having a child; I had never had a yes before. When I was fifteen, the doctor gave me, "You'll have problems ever conceiving." The doctor who started me on the fertility drugs had given me, "This could help." The IVF specialist gave me percentages of possibilities, and of course the medium gave me a definitive, "No." But this, this was an actual plan, and I was keen to follow it.

So began my journey with God. I finally had a *yes!*

CHAPTER SIX

New Hope

I had hope again. I didn't know how it was going to happen or when it was going to happen, but I had hope that we would one day be a family.

Our marriage was pretty rocky. The move had taken the pressure off us for a while as we focussed on settling into our new life and Ian into his new job, but it didn't take long before our grief and loss caught up with us again. Our conversations revolved around our activities of daily living, like what time would we be home and what was for dinner. We rarely spoke about Michael or John, or our grief; we were tired of talking about it. What else was there left to say that hadn't already been said? Our words didn't change anything, and they were not helping us heal. We would go around in circles with the *what if's* and *why did that happen* scenarios which kept opening the wounds but didn't provide any soothing balm to our broken hearts. Things needed to change for us in a big way or we weren't going to make it through. When we were going through IVF the support group leader spoke about how infertile couples had an extremely high rate of separation and divorce and we didn't want to be in those statistics.

I really looked forward to going to church every week, I felt like the message was speaking directly to me. I started making friends and got involved with groups that would meet up outside of church. My preconceived ideas about who God was and how church functioned were being challenged. Growing up without a dad around had given me the experience that fathers did not care. After my parents divorced, I only saw my dad maybe five times in the next twelve years, and of those times, sometimes it was only for a couple of hours. He would call on our birthdays and at Christmas and tell us he loved us, then nothing until the next birthday came around. There was no action behind those words of love. I would read how God was my Father and how much He loved me, and I was very accepting of those statements. What I couldn't get my head around was that He wanted to know me and help me. Honestly, like, how was that supposed to happen?

There was another ladies' event at the church and the speaker was talking about pain and disappointment, she quoted this scripture: "Hope deferred makes the heart sick, but dreams fulfilled are the tree of life." Proverbs 13:12

Well, there you go. My dreams were certainly not fulfilled and my heart was definitely sick and here was this woman who did not know me or my circumstances, relating to what was going on inside me. My heart lit up, it showed me God understood my circumstances and understood why I was so angry. I was angry with myself as a woman and as a wife, I was so angry I was not able to have a child especially when so many others had no problems conceiving—outside of our fertility treatments we still had not met any other infertile couples. Then of course, I felt guilty I was angry. I just wanted to accept my situation, stop stressing about it and get on with our life. I was grieving for my dreams and could not let go. That is what happens after nearly ten years of disappointment. I needed healing and hearing that scripture had started the healing process.

Whether it was true or not, I felt that no one really understood what we were going through and here was God saying, *"Yes, that's right. It's okay that you're angry, that's what happens when dreams don't happen the way you expect them to."* He just kept putting things in front of me, showing me it was okay I was feeling that way. I realised I felt guilty about feeling this way, thinking my feelings weren't normal, but they were normal. Of course, this was the first step in the healing process.

I couldn't stay in this place of being justified that my feelings were okay, it was the place I had to start from and take it one step at a time. God had hold of me now and would stay with me through the healing of my heart and body. He took me on a journey of His love, His grace, and His mercy. Things got incredibly hard at times, but in all the years I never felt God leave me.

Ian was quite surprised when I started going to church as he had never known me to go before, it was not something he had ever really considered for his own life either. After about eighteen months he could see the difference in me. Although I still had moments of stress and angst, I stopped being so fully consumed and was now only partially consumed by us not having kids. Ian decided to start coming to church as well.

We were doing life together again and we were doing church together, our relationship was on the up again. We now had a newfound love of something we could do and talk about that wasn't revolving around kids and lack of kids. We started attending a Bible study the church put on, as Ian said, "Best to learn about what I believe in now."

We had a visiting minister come to preach and he asked those that wanted to, to come up the front and ask for one thing and he would pray with them. I remember I went up the front and the minister said to me, "What do you want?"

"I want to have a baby," I replied.

He didn't say no. He prayed for us to have a child because nothing is impossible with God.

I couldn't help but notice the similarities from when I attended the spiritual meeting when I had been given a definitive *'No'* to having a baby, but it was the differences that counted. Instead of negativity and annoyance I was given a hope filled answer. That's what God is...Hope. Jesus is our Hope, our hope for the future. I came home and I was elated. I thought, *this is it. I'll be pregnant any day now.*

I wasn't.

I was crushed again. I could not understand it because I had been getting a *yes*. A yes from God. A *yes, it's going to happen. Yes, I'm going to give you a child. Yes. Let's pray about it.* Like, people would gather around me, they would be praying and I would be hearing *yes*. I was so devastated. I had allowed my heart to go to that place of hope that it was going to happen. I laid in bed sobbing with Ian next to me, him devastated as well, asking me to please stop crying. He could not take the sadness anymore. I then felt a peace fall over me and my whole body relaxed; it was like I was being hugged. The peace of God enveloped me, I felt like I was being wrapped up in a big, comfy, soft doona. I knew everything was going to be okay. I stayed in bed for about an hour before I felt ready to get up and get on with my day.

I started working in the church office doing administration and helping in the services. One particular morning I was running around for the minister giving the message when the comment was made, "Leanne, you can always be my altar girl."

I sat down, blown away. No one knew what happened when I was fourteen so to have this statement made to me, I knew it had to of come directly from God. He knew I had wanted to serve in the church and was happy I was there doing it.

On another occasion a visiting minister came, he heard about our story and called us both up for prayer. He prayed, saying, "Within twelve months you'll be pregnant."

Again, we had something new to hope for and for twelve months we hung onto that. Almost twelve months later to the day, I still wasn't pregnant. I remember being so crushed again, but it was a different sort of crush. I was disappointed, but in my heart there was still that place of hope—it was more of a *not yet* than a *no*. I was hanging onto that *yes* in my heart, but I was getting tired of being the infertile woman; there was more to me than that.

I felt I had reached saturation point. I didn't want to talk about kids, the lack of my own or the presence of other peoples. If I was standing with a group and the conversation turned to their children and what was happening in their lives I would just walk away. I had nothing to contribute to the conversation. My circle of friends was getting smaller. Ian and I decided to hang out with older couples as they had already had their families. For us, other than the fact these were beautiful people, it was a matter of self-preservation and the preservation of our friends. If we were not being faced constantly with others achieving their dreams, we were not going to be triggered as much and others would not have to suffer through the tears of our pain.

I found myself running around trying to please people. I was looking for my place in the community to give me a reason why I was here. I would say *yes* to just about everything. If I was not going to be being a mum, then maybe I was going to be the greatest support person around. Not that I had any real training in that, but I ran around helping all the time. I didn't want to think about what I wanted or needed in my life. Experience taught me it didn't matter because I wasn't going to achieve my dreams. I would find fulfillment helping others. So, that was what I did. It was not the healthiest approach to my life, but it was safer for my broken heart.

I also needed to work out a way to deal with my desires convincing my mind I was pregnant. I found myself constantly looking for signs to confirm my hopes...

Oh, I have an ache in my boobs, I must be pregnant.

Oh, my period is three seconds late, I must be pregnant.

Oh, I'm feeling a bit sick this morning, I must be pregnant.

I would spiral up and down in this state of excitement, angst, trepidation and hope. I honestly thought I was going crazy.

When I got into this mindset I couldn't function. It began around the second year of trying to fall pregnant and if I could distract myself with other things filling my life, such as fostering or moving or going on holidays, it was not as bad. These thoughts were fully heightened through the whole IVF process. It did not happen every month and as the years went on it occurred less and less. I would still have days when I completely convinced myself it finally happened and on those days I couldn't go out, I couldn't talk. I would lose my breath and on one or two occasions I almost fainted at the thought. I needed to find a solution so I could get my mind and body back on an even keel again. The solution I found was to take a pregnancy test. Once I did that and got the negative result, I was able to get on with my day, that was how I coped. For me, it was a positive way for me to reset my day and move on.

I also realised it was time to go back to counselling.

This was not the best way to live. The spiritual side of healing had started, but there was the mental and emotional side of things as well. I knew the importance of looking after myself and my own mental health. So, I went to counselling and it helped a lot. I was given lots of strategies and guidance on how to deal with the pain and disappointments, as well as strategies on what I could to do when I was being completely overwhelmed with grief. More issues surfaced that needed healing, which I was told was not an unusual occurrence when you go to counselling.

Overall, there's years of counselling; there's singular counselling by myself, then couples counselling with Ian. Lots of ideas I had about life and how I didn't deserve good things I discovered were false. Just because we found God didn't mean all our marital problems went away, or the conditions that caused the infertility were healed immediately. We had to deal with a whole heap of stuff. It was hard and emotional work, but we both wanted to have healing from our disappointments. It didn't take them away but what it did do was help put them in the right place. We learnt how to deal with the pain better and allow ourselves to not take on the guilt.

I was not the fun-loving girl Ian married and he was not the same man I married, and that was normal. We were both putting pressure on the other to be the same, to react in the same way to a situation, just as we had done at the start of our relationship. It could be hard to put that into a framework of our life, it was an easy concept to think about but sometimes our sub conscientious didn't agree. Learning these concepts and understanding and accepting our reality, was what brought a lot of peace and healing to our lives. So we did counselling on our marriage, we did counselling on our infertility, and we both had singular counselling. We were not perfect—still aren't. Stuff happened and we needed to learn how to cope with the things that came to beat us up over our life.

One thing I have learnt from counselling is that if you think you may need it, go and have counselling. If it takes a while to find the right counsellor, do not stop looking. Try a couple of different counsellors until you find the right fit for you, then go see them. Allow yourself to find the healing you need in life. I discovered I was punishing myself because I thought all the things that happened in my life must have been my fault somehow and I deserved it. Counselling helped me realise that was a lie, and maybe it's a lie you have been listening to as well.

CHAPTER SEVEN

Possibly Adoption?

Ian had started his own business about twelve months after we moved north, doing interiors for catamarans being built in the local area. It was a one man show and he loved being his own boss. It took about a year per boat to complete so we weren't making a lot of profit, but Ian enjoyed the work.

We were about thirty-six and had been living in the area about four years at that time when we decided that maybe adoption could work for us, so we started looking into the process. We travelled to Sydney for an information night only to be informed that adoption in Australia was and is very different to adoption in a lot of other countries. It is more difficult and expensive and can take years. At the time we were informed that there were twelve babies born here available to be adopted in the whole of Australia. A population of over twenty-million people and there were only twelve babies. Even adopting through the foster care system was not a guarantee at the time and we were not prepared to put ourselves through that process again with no definite assurance we would be able to adopt. This was around the mid-2000s at the time, so thank goodness for the sake of the children and other foster parents hoping to adopt, that the fostering to adoption laws have changed since then, making the process easier.

Overseas adoption was looking like our only option. There was a minimum wait of two years that could blow out to seven and with the cut off age of adopting parents being forty, we needed to get a move on. We signed up to start the process and found out it was going to cost a minimum of $25,000. Both parents needed to be able to travel overseas to pick the child up and we could be in the adoptive country for a couple of weeks. The countries the children were coming from not only took the age of the prospective parents into consideration, but also their finances, health, and weight. Obviously on paper this looked like it was a good thing, but reality rarely matches up with paper statistics. These rules allow for the child to remain in an overseas orphanage with all the horrors that can be attached to that, rather than be adopted with a possibility that one of the adoptive parents may suffer ill health. We had no concerns over the police checks that were required, but I know from personal experience, many of the prerequisites slow the process and exclude families that would make great parents. We were accepted into the program with our only option in the process being to adopt from China as we were not considered wealthy or healthy enough to fulfill the criteria of other countries. We allowed ourselves to get a little excited about the thought of adopting, but it was going to be a long process and we had been disappointed before.

We were waiting on all the police and community checks to be done and to hear back about the next stage of the process when the Global Financial Crisis hit, devastating the boatbuilding industry. One of the first things people stop buying when they are financially stressed is luxury items, like catamarans. Basically, the bottom fell out of our business and the finances were no longer available for us to do the adoption.

We were faced with yet another *no*.

It had been fifteen years of *no*.

No, you can't have your own child.

No, fertility treatments and IVF aren't going to work for you either.

How about fostering? *No*.

Adoption? *No*.

We resigned ourselves to being the infertile couple. We were getting off the rollercoaster and shutting the circus down. The freak show was over and the star attractions had closed the curtains. Enough was enough. Fifteen years was enough.

And back into counselling I go.

CHAPTER EIGHT

Secret Hope

So why did I still have hope? Hope that stayed hidden in my heart, deep down, that no one else could see. I had been given a promise and I was not letting go of it. I just decided not to share it anymore.

Things had certainly improved within our marriage and our relationship was back on track. Anyone who has been married for any length of time would know that even within the best of marriages, you have your ups and downs and we had certainly worked hard on our marriage to keep us together. We had basically put our disappointments to the side, not forgotten but to the side, so we could move forward with our life. They were there if we needed to talk about them, but they could no longer be at the forefront of our lives anymore. Neither of us had given up on the promise from God, it had been nearly eight years since we first gave our hearts to Jesus and seven years since we were told we would be pregnant in twelve months. We had done all we could do, so now it was time to stand on God's word.

For the next few years, we lived our life. We closed the business down and focussed on paying off debt. Ian had gone back to paid employment and we were both heading towards forty. I was actually excited about turning forty as it meant I was leaving my childbearing years behind me. I was now heading to an age that I would no longer be asked when I would be having kids; the older you get the less people tend to ask those questions. I had a fabulous fortieth birthday and not long after that started a new job that used both my administration and nursing skills. Life had definitely improved.

I still loved God and loved going to church, my relationship with Jesus deepened. Realising and accepting that having a relationship with God was not like a wishing well, I was not there to direct Him but the other way round. God wanted the best for me and directed my life through His Word, I trusted Him. In saying that, Ian and I both agreed we did not want our infertility to be so obvious in our church life. If we wanted someone to pray for us we waited until after the church service was over to get prayer. If we had visiting ministry in the church, I would sit in the sound booth with Ian so I would not get called out. We knew God hadn't forgotten us; I had a place in my heart where I hung onto the promise with everything inside me.

Whenever I would get caught up about the length of time we had been on this path to parenthood, God reminded me of all the people in the Bible that waited years for their promise to come to fruition. Like Joseph, he was a teenager when God gave him the dream of his future as a powerful ruler that even his brothers and father would bow to. But it didn't happen straight away and the journey for him seemed to go in the opposite direction of the dream. He was thrown in a pit, then sold into slavery, was falsely accused of rape and ended up in jail for years before the pharaoh heard about his gift for deciphering dreams and ended up making him the ruler of Egypt. Years spent seemingly going in the opposite direction of the dream before it came into being.

I also believe God has a special place for women who can't have babies, there are stories after stories recounting the plight of these women and how God was with them. I think in the different stages of my journey I experienced most of these emotions; the desperation of Hannah as she went up onto the altar, crying hysterically. Her desperation was so bad the priest thought she was drunk; but she was crying out to God in all her pain and anguish, unable or not wanting to hide her pain.

There was the woman who the built the room for Elijah who hid her face when Elijah asked her what she wanted. I believe she did that because she didn't want to think about her desire to have a son. Didn't want to get her hopes up. I recognised that feeling; not wanting to go to the place of where you have so much hope only to have it dashed again. You end up being too frightened to speak it out loud, to look at the possibility. Continued disappointment brought pain, so she hid her face in the doorframe. She got her son, as did Hannah who ended up having quite a few children.

Sarah, Abraham's wife, waited for years. She was well past childbearing age when Abraham was again told his descendants would be as many as the stars in the sky. This was not the first time she had heard this promise. So many had told her she would have a child when she was still young enough to conceive. But she was now in her nineties, and she laughed. She laughed at the thought of it because the idea was so preposterous; if it was going to happen, it would of by now. God did not tell her she was wrong for not having faith, He understood. God understood her pain and disbelief. That was the part of Sarah's story that resounds in my heart. I understood her laughter too.

It was easy to get caught up in the idea that because we were Christians we had to be perfect and therefore our life would be perfect. But that in itself was a lie. God was big enough to handle our pain, our grief, and even our anger. God did not expect perfect, He was wanting our hearts to be honest with Him, no pretence required. The number of times I called out to Him when I was in the shower were too many to count. The shower became my place to cry, vent my anger, be vulnerable and show my heart.

One day I was reading scripture and I read this passage; Proverbs 30:15:

> *"There are four things in life that are never satisfied;*
> *Death;*
> *Wildfire;*
> *Drought;*
> *Infertility."*

Yes! I thought. There it was, exactly how I felt. Each of these things are all encompassing. There is nothing you can do about them. There is nothing you can change. Death, yes, that is final and all encompassing. When there's drought, there's no food or water and it often brings death. A wildfire, like a massive bushfire, is something we have a lot of in Australia, and when the wildfire comes through it absolutely destroys everything in its path. It's all consuming and each of these things takes our focus away from anything and everything else, including God.

And the fourth thing is a barren woman, infertility.

Infertility is just as consuming as all these massive life changing events that hold our attention away from everything else.

I read this scripture and stopped in my tracks, and I read it again. Suddenly I had this massive revelation that God truly understood exactly where I was at and exactly how I felt. This infertility was like this big black cloud hanging over me all the time. No matter what I did, no matter where I went, no matter what I said, everything I did came from the place of my distress over infertility.

As I read this scripture again, I realised this was the thing holding me back and I started jumping for joy. It was a massive thing; the big black cloud just fell off me. I finally understood. God understood me, He understood me at the beginning of my journey when my heart was so sick and He understood me now. He understood my fears and desires, He saw me as an individual, He knew exactly the pain I was feeling. He loved me. There was nothing holding me back from Him now. I could not keep putting my loss and pain between myself and all my relationships, especially my relationship with God. He held onto me and helped move the mountain blocking my way so I could finally move forward. This is the moment, I believe, God finished His healing work in me around my infertility.

Not long after this Ian invited me out to lunch. It was very formal for him, so I knew he had something to talk about; something important. I also knew not to push him for the conversation, thinking, *he's got something on his mind and he needs to tell me in his own way.* All week he kept reminding me of our lunch date. The weekend finally came around and he took me to a little cafe on a peninsula that was very private, where we found a table away from the other patrons there. I had no idea what he wanted to talk about, but I was starting to worry; worry that he had some terrible news.

He started talking about our journey; how hard it had been for him, how he was sorry for all that had happened to us and how he had shut himself down. My eyes started leaking, Ian was getting death stares from the other tables—they couldn't hear our conversation, they could only see him talking and me crying—but he ignored them and continued.

"Maybe we could look into the adoption route again?" he said quietly.

"Yes, maybe we could," I agreed.

It was the 27th of June 2010 and the decision was made to try adopting again.

CHAPTER NINE

Two Lines

It was a Friday in July 2010 and I was not feeling the best. My period had been four weeks late, which wasn't unusual, then finally arrived with a vengeance; I was in so much pain. A week went by and my period was lasting a lot longer than usual which was quite strange. I was being woken up at night because my boobs were incredibly sore. I still had my period, so I didn't think I was pregnant, but my whole body felt *weird*. I put it down to starting menopause. But the pain and weird feelings were not going away so I started talking myself into the possibility of being pregnant. My brain went into the usual spin, something that had not happened in years. I recognised where my brain was taking me so it was time to take a test and get myself back on an even keel. Ian had already left for work, so I went in and took the pregnancy test.

Now I probably have taken hundreds of tests over the years, sometimes four or five tests in the space of two days if my obsession was at its peak, so I was an expert. None of this *leave it and come back in ten minutes to check the result.* That went out the window years earlier.

I was watching the liquid move up the results window. A line came, appearing in the wrong spot. I was looking at it, thinking, *that's weird, they've moved the negative line.* Then the second line appeared. *There are two lines*, I thought. *Two lines!* I was just sitting there not really understanding what I was looking at. I was confused, wondering, what did this mean? I knew what it meant I just couldn't comprehend it. *It's impossible, but it can't be impossible because I'm looking at it.* I picked up the phone and called Ian.

"Two Lines," was all I could say.

"What?"

"Two lines," I repeated

Complete silence on the other end of the phone, then, "Really?"

"Yes, two lines!" I exclaimed; they were the only words I was managing to get out.

We were both in complete shock.

I got myself together and went to work. The only thing running through my head all day was *two lines*. But I didn't think it was real, that there must be some sort of mistake. When I got home that afternoon we tried to get to the doctors, but it was too late in the day. We tried a clinic on Saturday morning, but we couldn't get in without waiting for hours. We resigned ourselves to waiting until Monday. We needed time to think about this; time to process what we thought was happening. We kept it to ourselves, thinking it was not real, as stupid as that sounds. I was still bleeding at the time, so we weren't even sure what was going to happen.

Monday came quickly, we both took the day off work and arrived at the doctors. I was hanging onto the pregnancy test, unable to let it go. My usual doctor was unavailable, so we were seeing someone new; a doctor that didn't know anything about us. We went in and I couldn't speak, Ian did most of the talking. I put the pregnancy test on her desk, and sat down looking at her. Ian explained everything that had been going on, she rang the ultrasound place and got me an appointment in two hours. It was the earliest I could have as I needed to drink lots of water to prepare for the ultrasound.

I was so confused, I had been bleeding for over a week now, so if I was experiencing a miscarriage I shouldn't be getting a positive pregnancy test result and how could I be pregnant if I was bleeding so much? Confusion reigned and answers were required! After two hours and two litres of water, we walked in and I said to the ultrasound technician, "The doctor says you have to tell me everything that's going on."

And he just looked at me with a smile that told me most of his patients say that and he asks, "Why? What do you think is going on?"

Ian explained everything again. I still couldn't put it into words.

While the technician was setting up to do the ultrasound, he was talking and says, "I know exactly how you feel. It took my wife and I eleven years to fall pregnant." He was the perfect technician for us, one who understood how we were feeling.

At the start of the ultrasound, we couldn't see the screen, then the next thing, he turned it around and said, "There's the little fellow." And right there was our tiny baby with a heart beating like crazy. *Boom, boom, boom*! I was overcome, Ian was overcome, we couldn't believe what we were seeing. *Thank You Jesus!* I thought.

He continued examining me, to find the source of the bleeding. He discovered an empty sack and said, "This happens to a lot of women your age." He explained, "You don't need to worry because your baby is fine." Relief washed over me. At the time I didn't think about what that empty sack actually meant, all I could think about was we were finally pregnant. Nearly ten weeks pregnant in fact.

Ten weeks!

We realised this meant I was pregnant the afternoon Ian took me to lunch! Ian was full of confidence and wanted to tell everyone. We rang our families; it was the most incredible and exciting news that we shared. We had so many different reactions; screams of joy and laughter, even stunned silence. Our family who walked the entire journey with us, supporting us, sharing our hopes and disappointments, were now sharing our elation and shock that is has finally happened. I don't think we all had laughed together so much in years. It was that joyous, excited laughing of shared love for a miracle. It was the day before my forty-second birthday.

News travelled fast, Ian told everyone he saw, I wanted to wait another two weeks before we told anybody else, just in case. It was a real role reversal of our personalities. The excitement was infectious, we could hardly believe it was real! An announcement was made at church and our church family who had been praying for ten years for this broke out in cheers and praise for our gracious God. This could only be described as a miracle. God had healed my body, there was no other explanation.

We decided we didn't want to know the gender of the baby; we had waited this long to fall pregnant so what was another six months. I had to go to the hospital on a weekly basis until the doctors were convinced the danger period was over—because I was still bleeding—which was around the fifteenth week. Every week I got to listen to the heartbeat and see our baby on the portable ultrasound machine. It was such a blessing and helped put my mind at ease. This particular day the doctor was looking for the baby's heartbeat to make sure everything was okay, and we saw this little baby spinning and spinning and spinning, then suddenly the baby stopped, looked straight up and waved. This is my favourite memory of being pregnant.

When we first went shopping, I didn't want to buy anything, thinking I was going to jinx it or something, but Ian kept picking things up, saying, "How about this?" and "Can I buy that?"

"Not yet, we're just looking at the moment, working out what we might need." I still didn't want to get too excited.

Ian disappeared and came back a while later with a giant teddy. "I don't care what you say, I'm buying this!" You couldn't wipe the smile from his face, it was the happiest I had seen him in the longest time. I allowed myself to get a baby cutlery set.

When we reached twenty weeks I finally started to relax. It was looking like parenthood was actually going to happen!

Ian built the baby a chest of drawers with the change table on the top and we set the room up with a white sign that said *BELIEVE* in capital letters over the cot. Believe that if God makes you a promise, it will happen.

I continued with the hospital visits and news of the pregnancy ran throughout the hospital. So many staff couldn't believe our story and would often come over to ask questions about length of time it took and if it was really *natural*. I also had quite a few people outside of the hospital ask if it was really Ian's baby, thinking I must have been with someone else and that was why I was finally pregnant! I used to laugh at these comments as most people didn't know it was me with the fertility problems not Ian.

The pregnancy went well, all things considered. Due to my age I had what is called a *geriatric pregnancy*, which I found funny because we started trying to have kids nice and young at twenty-four, and now at forty-two it was finally happening, I get to have a geriatric pregnancy! I ended up with gestational diabetes as well and luckily managed to get over my phobia of injecting myself because of it. Due to this I needed to leave work earlier than expected, but overall it was a great experience.

The baby shower was huge with family and friends travelling to celebrate. I could hardly believe this was happening and that all these people were here to celebrate our impending birth. I thought I would never of had this opportunity and here it was, happening. There were a few moments when the emotion overwhelmed me—I couldn't read the cards on the day, the words kept getting blurred for some reason!

I was getting used to being stared at when I was out and began to realise it was not often you saw an older woman pregnant. When I was nearly eight months pregnant, I was in town with a friend when this stranger started towards me.

"What are you doing! What are you thinking?" she yelled as she approached me. "You're crazy having a baby at your age!"

I was really surprised this woman thought she could comment so intensely over my pregnancy, especially since I didn't know her at all. I simply turned and gave her the biggest smile and replied, "It's my first and it's taken eighteen years to fall pregnant, I'm very happy it's happening."

Her horror at my old age pregnancy turned around straight away, although she did have to clarify that she wouldn't be happy if it was her!

I loved being pregnant. In all honesty I was so grateful that I finally got to have this experience and couldn't wait to meet our child.

CHAPTER TEN

God Remembered

So here we were nearing the end of our pregnancy, it wouldn't be long now. The baby was breech, meaning our little fellow was facing up instead of down. As we were looking forward to a natural birth we hoped our baby would turn...but that wasn't to be. As it was a geriatric pregnancy with gestational diabetes and the baby breech, the doctors made the decision I would be having a caesarean as that was the safest delivery option for both of us. The baby was due on the 20th of February 2011 and I was booked in for the caesarean eleven days earlier. I was disappointed, but not really; nothing could take my joy away. If that was how it had to be, okay, we get to meet our baby earlier.

Excitement was running high as the day approached. Family arrived, we had friends come over the night before going into hospital, talking about the changes that were about to happen. We would be leaving the house tomorrow as a couple and returning as a family. Our life was about to change forever.

Three days after our eighteenth wedding anniversary, Ian and I headed into the hospital together. Today was the day!

As far as I knew, I would be having a spinal block and be awake for the birth with Ian right beside me. We were filled with high anticipation. The pre-op preparation began, photos were taken, we prayed together, then Ian went to get his scrubs on. I was then wheeled into the anaesthetic room before going into the operation theatre.

Final questions were asked, "Have you ever had a back injury?"

"Yes, I have," I replied.

The nurse got up and left the room and came back with the anaesthetist. He asked about what sort of injury I had, and after some discussion he said to me, "I'm not willing to give you a spinal block. If I do you could end up as a paraplegic. You'll need to have a general anaesthetic."

My heart sank. If I was going to go under a full general anaesthetic, I would be asleep and no family would be allowed in the operating theatre which meant Ian would also miss it too. I remember looking at Ian so disappointed that we would both miss the birth. I wanted to take the chance, confident that it would all be okay. The anaesthetist gave us some time to discuss our decision alone, he and the staff left the room.

Ian and I talked about it…well, Ian did most of the talking. He already knew I wanted to take the chance. Ian wasn't willing to take the risk though, he wanted me to have the general anaesthetic.

The anaesthetist returned and asked if we had made our decision.

"Yes, we have. I'll have the general anaesthetic," I said. "But before we go any further, I need you to understand something. It has taken us eighteen years to get to this precise moment. Neither of us have been in this place before and I'm upset that now we're both going to miss it."

The anaesthetist looked at me, then he looked up at Ian and said, "You'll be right, won't you mate? You won't faint or anything?"

"Yep, I'll be right," Ian replied with a giant grin.

And they let him in!

So, Ian got to come in and see the birth of our child. He got to cut the umbilical cord and was the first to hold our precious baby. The next thing I remember was waking up and wondering where I was and what just happened. The memory flooded in, *oh that's right, I'm having a baby.* I looked around; Ian was next to me holding my hand.

"What did we have?" I asked.

"A boy and he's beautiful, he's with the nurses in neonatal ICU right now."

We had a boy. A beautiful boy. I went to back to sleep and when I woke back in our room, the nurse brought my baby in and gave him to me. It was the most surreal moment of my life. This was my son Zachariah. Zachariah, which means *God remembered*, and he was the most beautiful child I had ever seen. God said *yes* and kept His promise. We were finally parents.

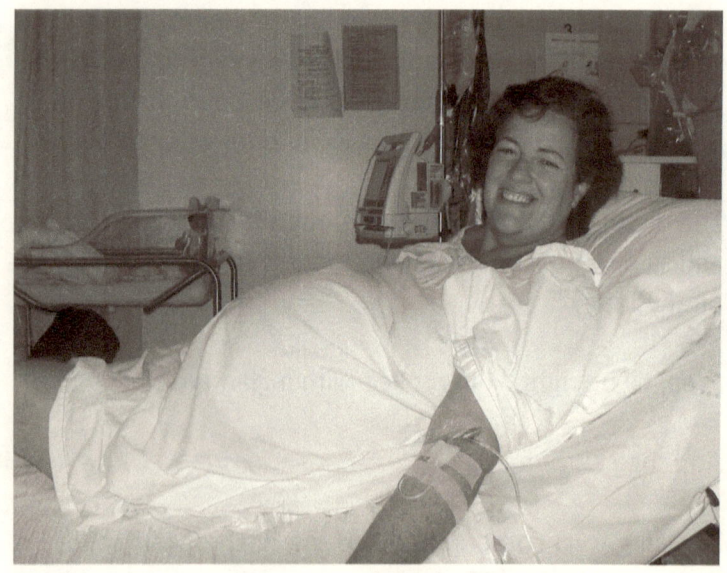

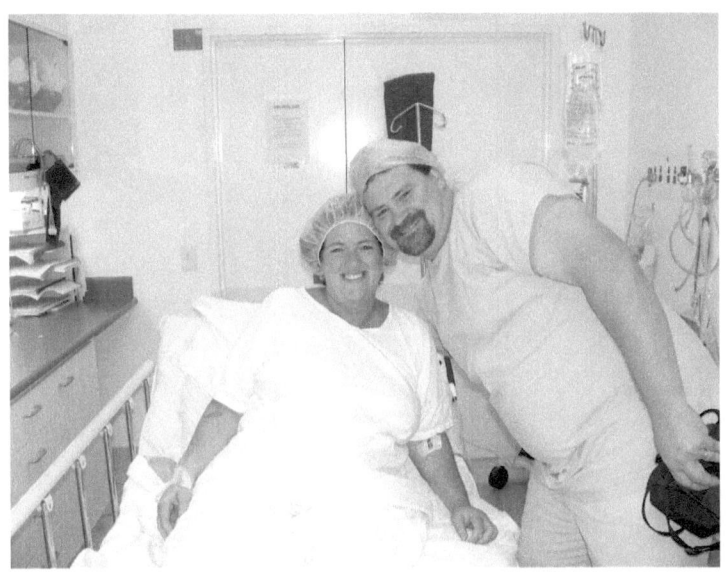
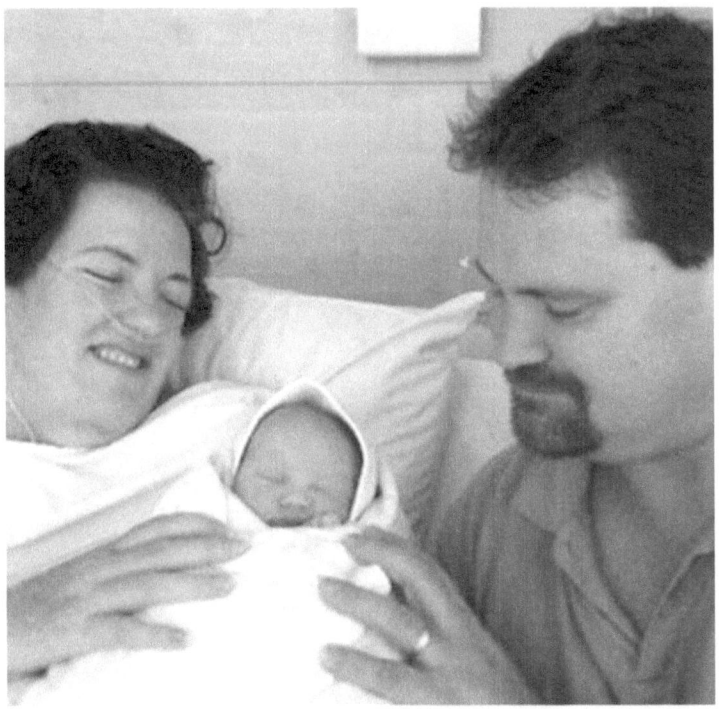

CHAPTER ELEVEN

Coming Home

I was completely in love with our little man with his wonky, misshaped head from being breech and the cutest button nose. Smokey blue eyes that would eventually turn brown and he was bald with the faintest red fuzz over his scalp. He was perfect. I was lucky enough to be able to breastfeed, although it did take a good six weeks or more for my nipples to stop complaining!

Ian was there every day doting on us both and although the caesarean was painful I had no complications and recovered well. So many people shared our joy. We received flowers and cards, some from the parents of our friends whom we had never even met, to congratulate us. The news of the miracle spread like wildfire. There was a nurse who asked if she could feature our story in her podcast. We had doctors come in, who weren't our doctors, to hear about our journey. It was a lovefest of joy!

After five days it was finally time to go home, Ian came to pick us up and we headed out to the car, it was drizzling rain a little and it felt like we were in a dream. We felt so blessed to be able to have these experiences. We may have been in our forties, but we were just like all the other couples bringing their baby home for the first time. There was excitement, joy, and a little bit of healthy fear. Age was only a number.

My mum and my twin sister had arrived for the birth, with Mum staying for a few weeks after to help out, whilst my twin headed home with her two youngest kids, all happy that they got to meet their cousin. I could not drive for six weeks and Ian went back to work after two weeks, so it was great having Mum around to help out. Lots of our friends from church brought us meals which made things so much easier as I was still recovering from the caesarean.

My in-laws arrived a few weeks later with more cousins to meet and the excitement continued. Ian and I went out to dinner; who would have thought that this was now going to be a rare opportunity after so long of it being just the two of us.

We started to get into a routine. Ian would come home every afternoon and give Zachariah his bath, he wanted to be as involved as much as he could and as I was breastfeeding there really wasn't a lot he could do in the beginning. I think I only bathed Zachariah maybe twice until he was two. I joined three different local Mum's groups and socialised Zach a lot. I knew he would be an only child—although I was hoping for another one—so I wanted him to be comfortable around people.

When Zach was about six months old, we organised to have him dedicated at church, similar to a christening, the difference being that Zach will have the choice of being water baptised when he grows up if he wants too. As his parents, we were promising to teach him about Jesus and allow him to make his own choice. Our ministers that had walked the last ten years with us had moved on to another church not long after we found out we were expecting, but we wanted them to do the service. One had had a vision of dedicating our baby years before we fell pregnant, and she had held onto that vision in confidence and prayer that God would keep His promise.

Family and friends came from near and far to celebrate with us. It was a beautiful service, the joy in the room was palpable. One comment made by a member of the church was that it was the longest and best dedication service they had ever been to!

The excitement levels eventually dropped and day to day routines took over. Babies are tiring and exhausting, especially when they are teething and not sleeping. I was tired and stressed and felt guilty that I was stressed. I thought, *I shouldn't be stressed, I should be grateful.* A very wise friend put my mind at ease:

"The miracle wasn't a perfect baby, Leanne. The miracle was your healing so you could have him, all mothers feel this way at some time or another. It is normal to feel tired. You're being too hard on yourself."

It's good to have wise friends around you.

I wanted to be a stay-at-home mum as much as I could, I felt I had waited so long for this little man I didn't want to miss anything if I could help it. I did start working part-time, one day a week when he was sixteen months old at a new job as my previous job didn't offer part-time. I put Zachariah into family day-care and he loved being around kids his own age. At eighteen months old Zachariah decided he no longer required an afternoon nap. He had always been an early riser, if he slept until 6am I considered it a sleep in. I tried everything to get him to keep his nap but the day I put him in the car and drove for nearly two hours with him singing happily in the back was the day I realised it was not going to happen. Nap time was done. It took a while to get used to no-sleeping-baby-breaks during the day, but the positive was he went to bed early and slept through most nights. Even when he started preschool, he didn't need a daytime sleep. The teachers gave him a book and he would happily lay on the camp cot surrounded by sleeping kids, reading.

A couple of weeks before Zach turned two he started climbing out of his cot, luckily we had a convertible cot that we could remove the sides on. From that moment he was determined to stay up and the bedtime battles began. It took a good six months of standing in his doorway, putting him back to bed, or lying-in bed with him before he gave up and went to bed without the fight.

Just a normal kid.

18 YEARS IN THE MAKING FOR THIS CHILD WE PRAYED

CHAPTER TWELVE

Cross Generational Connections

Sometimes I struggle with the thought of Zachariah being an only child, with old parents. We had hoped for at least one more, but it wasn't meant to be. Ian and I are grateful we were lucky enough to have him. Throughout the eighteen years we have met other couples who never achieved their dream of a child, and I have been inspired by their steadfastness with each other and the ability to put their anguish aside in order to move forward with their lives. We have also met many more whose marriages didn't last, remarrying to achieve their dream of becoming parents or just having the pain and disappointment drive them apart. I can understand both scenarios as I was willing to let Ian go so he could become a father.

Being an older parent has a unique set of experiences that we have learnt to laugh about; being mistaken for grandparents would be at the top of the list. One amusing scenario occurred when Zachariah was about three, we were in a coffee shop in our local town when the people at the next table struck up a conversation.

"Aren't grandkids the best, especially when you get to hand them back."

We laughed and agreed with them as we had found that trying to explain our situation took the conversation to a deeper level that we weren't always willing to go into, nor was the person making the conversation interested in. We laughed together and accepted the compliments on how gorgeous our grandson was when Zach piped up:

"Mum, I need to go."

Oops, the ruse was over!

Being mistaken for the grandparents wasn't always met with laughter though. There were times when we wanted the automatic recognition, like when I needed to take him to the emergency room with croup or for a sprained ankle when he got a bit older. My parental identity has always needed explanation.

There was also the time when I was picking Zach up from school and one of the teachers, who was not one of Zach's regulars, announced, "Zach your nanna is here."

I am not angry with these comments. With the roles reversed there's a good chance I would be saying the same thing, but sometimes it would be nice to have the automatic recognition from strangers.

Being in mother's groups was also an interesting experience, there was only one other older mum in her forties in one group I went to, but the rest of the women were at least ten to fifteen years younger than me, some even younger. I was the same age or only a couple of years younger than quite a few of the women's own mums. I would have some of the toddlers call me *nanna* and when the women talked about the latest music or TV shows they liked I was at a loss. I rarely knew the songs or musicians and my TV and movie likes were completely different. The bonuses were, they taught me about social media and how to use it and translated the latest words, lingo and crazes for me. I explained history! Not really just a little exaggeration. The positives of our newfound relationships far outweighed any negatives with the opportunity being given to me to get to know this generation better, which honestly, probably wouldn't have happened otherwise. I consider myself now almost fluent in cross generational discussions…sometimes.

I also never thought that I would be a helicopter parent but discovered this trait in myself one day at the park with a group of mums and their kids. I found myself yelling, "Be careful, be careful, watch what you're doing." I was full of angst that some major tragedy was about to happen. I looked up and realised all the other mums were sitting together, enjoying a chat while I was carrying on like a pork chop. It took lots of practise to sit myself down and allow Zach to play. We all have our struggles.

All these things are inconsequential to the large story and minor hiccups in our day-to-day life. It is a life I never expected to have. I finally found my *normal*.

Zachariah is an independent kid who knows what he wants. He has a huge heart and adores his family and friends. He loves music and singing and has started to learn the saxophone. Our hopes for him are to not get caught up in what others or society pressures consider *normal* in life. We know *normal* is different for everyone and really, as I once read, it is just a setting on the washing machine. We hope he finds his own personal relationship with God and never fears stepping out to try new things. We hope he understands that life is not always fun, but there will be joy as well as trials and struggles, the need to sometimes fight hard for what you want in life and never be afraid to ask for help. Also, the wisdom to know when to let things go and move onto something new. We don't mind what he wants to do as a profession as long as he is happy doing it. That's all we can do for him, as his parents, to teach him about God and life as we know it, then the choices will be his.

I thank God every day that we have been given this opportunity.

CROSS GENERATIONAL CONNECTIONS

Thoughts From Ian

The first time I saw Leanne I knew she was the woman for me; she was beautiful, still is. She was sitting in the snooker room and I thought, *there's the girl I'm going to marry.* So I did.

The journey towards having a child is not easy for many men. It often means re-establishing the way we look at life and those around us with a view to being more outwardly focused. It was that way for me in my journey with Leanne, I just had a lot more time than most men, to get my head around the thought of being a father.

I found IVF was one long disappointment with limited chance of success, it was especially hard on Leanne being treated like a medical experiment with all the injections and procedures she had to have. I tried to be there for her when we got another negative result, not worrying about how I was feeling; I was trying to help her get through it the best I could. I hated how it changed our life and our love life, we couldn't just enjoy each other anymore with our times together having to be scheduled.

I enjoyed fostering, the kids were great and I thought we were doing something that would really help them have a better life but found there were too many issues and agendas from others, family members and DOCS, that got in the way of the kids' best interests for their lives. I thought it was more about ticking the right boxes than the welfare of the kids, I wouldn't do it again.

As I recall, it was around the time Zach was born that a wise man we both knew said to me, "Love is an action not just a feeling." This was the state of mind I had been trying to make real in our lives for many years at that point without actually putting it into words. We showed each other our love with our actions. The initial feelings we had for each other had been moved aside, not lost, but were to be overtaken by the monthly reminder that we may never have children. I can recall the sinking of my heart every time Leanne got her period because of the pain she felt every time the hope she had was not fulfilled. I didn't express how I was feeling when that reminder came each month, I was too worried about Leanne and her feelings to consider how it was really affecting me. I didn't allow myself to feel. As much as we both wanted the situation we were in to change, it was not in our hands. We put our love for each other into action the best way we knew how for so many years.

Leanne has always had the motherly heart towards children and adults alike. She has always known when someone needs a hug or a kind word. As most women are, relationships with others are important to them. I wasn't like that, I came to the realisation I probably wouldn't be a dad and tried to sink myself into work, it was the place where I had control over the things in my life and I didn't have to face the issues inside myself that were holding me back from relationships with almost everyone in my life, not just Leanne. As it seems to be in so many marriages the wife realises this a long time before the husband, which in itself leads to many and varied discussions in differing levels of volume and intensity. This revelation, whether I realised it myself or it was shown to me, led me to go into counselling.

This is where I learnt how to shift the focus from myself to those around me and more toward my lovely wife and our life together. The counselling didn't change the things that happened to me or around me or even because of me over the years, but it did help me to understand my reactions and responses and look at things in a different way. A journey I am still on.

The turning point in the *having a child* journey came when I was in this head space. I realised that I had kept the thought of having a child at a distance for a long time and I resolved to try and fix it, to step into the only way I could see a possibility of us becoming parents. I needed to talk to Leanne.

We went to lunch on a Sunday at the end of June. Leanne and I sat down, we needed to discuss some things. I explained that I understood I had been distant about the child topic, made mistakes and wanted to focus on adoption once again. There were tears from both of us, as we decided to put our energy toward the process of becoming part of a young child's life through what we felt was our only option left. I felt peace and resolved to make it happen, not knowing exactly how that would occur.

We didn't know it then, but Zach was already with us.

The day Leanne rang me at work and said to me 'two lines, two lines' was a day I will never forget. I was working in a boat yard at the time and had moved out the back of the shed to hear Leanne properly. As I wandered aimlessly around the empty 44 Gallon Drums haphazardly placed about, struggling to understand and then believe what she was saying. It was just before her forty-second birthday and the news that we were quite possibly, after all these years, about to be parents, was unbelievable to me. My head was saying, *you have been here before and it didn't end well*, but it felt different. We dared to believe and embarrassed ourselves over the next few months with the energy of twenty-year-old's—well maybe thirty-somethings—getting everything ready.

The day Zach was born was the single best day of my life. There were so many emotions, I couldn't put a name on them all. We knew it had to be a caesarean section birth, but as we were going in the anaesthetist said to us that Leanne would need a general anaesthetic. My emotions bottomed out as he said I could not be in the theatre with Leanne during the operation. Leanne voiced to him that we hadn't come all this way to have our child come into the world with an unconscious mother and a father in the waiting room. After our objections, the team of doctors and nurses were gracious enough to let me be part of the birth, for which I am forever grateful. I would not see the surgery but would be at Leanne's head during the birth. A wonderful nurse took photos and a video of the moment, giving us a lasting record of the entry of our child to the world.

Now, nothing I had done, learnt, felt, understood, encountered, or known to this point in my life, could have possibly prepared me for what was about to happen.

As Leanne lay on the operating table, I was at her head holding her hand, the doctor and nurses moved quite feverishly the other side of the screen that they had placed so I couldn't see what was going on. And then the moment was upon me. I saw a nurse take a small something from the mayhem and place that something in a clear plastic shape to my right, that until this point, I hadn't noticed. Now my attention was totally focused on this table/crib as another nurse joined her and quickly rubbed down the something with linen that was so incredibly white. One of them glanced my way and said, "It's a boy," which I didn't comprehend immediately. I had convinced myself for some time that our child was going to be a girl.

A pair of scissors were handed to me with the question, "Would you like to cut the umbilical cord?" Confusion entered my mind; I would have to let go of Leanne's hand to do this.

A nurse realised what was going on in my mind and without me saying anything, she said to me, "I'll hold her hand while you cut the cord."

I reluctantly let go of Leanne's hand and moved towards the small bundle. I knew the cord had already been cut once by the doctor, but I was given instruction on where to cut again and did so with no further thought, between the clamps as directed. I questioned the earlier statement—it's a boy—as the two nurses quickly wrapped the bundle up and then lifted the clean tightly wrapped package toward me saying, "Meet your son." I saw his face peeping through the wrapping, his eyes now closed, he was snug and looking cosy. I sat back down next to Leanne, taking her hand in my left hand, holding my son in my right hand, close to my chest.

I took a breath, not sure that I had done that for some time.

The activity continued on the other side of the screen as I tried to understand what was happening for us at that moment. I suddenly felt so utterly helpless, inadequate. The love of my life to my left, unconscious, being stitched back together and my just born child in my right hand, being the most vulnerable he will ever be in his life.

Never before have I been in a situation where I was so utterly not in control, emotion overwhelmed me as this understanding overtook me.

He's a boy. I had been convinced we were having a girl. A whole array of different thoughts, which to this point I had not considered, flooded my brain. *What will he look like?*

Will he like footy? Will he be good at maths? I had a son but my mind had been preparing for a daughter.

The time since these moments have been amazing. Now, having a family, we experience new things again with Zach, teaching and learning together as a new journey takes the place of the previous one. A new journey to impart the things we have learnt to a bright young mind who is thirsty for knowledge.

Love now has a whole new meaning.

Ian.

About The Author

Leanne Davey was born in Sydney, New South Wales, her childhood spent living in the Blue Mountains of New South Wales and Arnhem Land in the Northern Territory before settling down on the Central Coast in New South Wales for her teenage years.

Six weeks into Year 12 Leanne left school, leaving her family and friends, to train as an Enrolled Nurse on Sydney's North Shore. Leanne continued nursing for seventeen years, working on the wards as well as a stint as an anaesthetic nurse for two years, before a back injury ended her nursing career. She then moved into office administration.

Leanne met her future husband, Ian, in October 1991, and they were married in February 1993. The couple have walked the infertility journey together before being joined by their son, Zachariah, in 2011.

Leanne has had a dream to write a book most of her life. Writing has always been an escape, a way to get her thoughts straight and express herself, and this shows through in her writing style.

Leanne has a deep faith in Jesus and has attended the same church for over twenty years with her husband, and believes their son is a product of a miracle that healed her body.

After many years of being asked to write her journey, Leanne has finally put pen to paper, so to speak, and written the story of their faith filled steps to parenthood.

Leanne currently lives in far northern New South Wales with her husband, son and wolfhound, Dusty.

18 YEARS IN THE MAKING
For This Child We Prayed

Leanne Davey

is an engaging and humorous speaker, who has the uncanny knack of putting others at ease with her storytelling. She tells of her life events with a rawness and honesty that draws the audience in and allows them to identify with her shared experiences.

Leanne's experience with the grief caused by infertility and how she learnt to live in that place for 18 years, offers hope to others in a similar position, not just in dealing with infertility, but living with disappointment of unfulfilled dreams and expectations.

Leanne has a faith in God that supported her through the years and is able to express how her faith helped her in the everyday experiences of her life.

If you would like Leanne to speak at your next event you can email her at admin@leannedavey.com or through her website www.leannedavey.com

www.ingramcontent.com/pod-product-compliance
Lightning Source LLC
Chambersburg PA
CBHW020132130526
44590CB00040B/518